MW00626776

JENNIFER JORDAN CRUZ

broken places can become the
sweetest places

LIFEWISE BOOKS

Broken Places Can Become the Sweetest Places

JENNIFER JORDAN CRUZ

Copyright © 2018 Jennifer Jordan Cruz. All rights reserved. Except for brief quotations for review purposes, no part of this book may be reproduced in any form without prior written permission from the author.

Published by:

⚓ LIFEWISE BOOKS

PO BOX 1072
Pinehurst, TX 77362
LifeWiseBooks.com

Cover Design and Interior Layout | Yvonne Parks | PearCreative.ca
Cover Concept and Photography | Daniel Cruz

To contact the author:
JenniferJordanCruz.com

ISBN (Print): 978-1-947279-38-4

dedication

This book is dedicated to the one who has given me more love than I deserve—that's my Jesus Christ!

To the love of my life and my hero, my husband Daniel Cruz: You have walked with me through my darkest moments; now together we will laugh forever. I love you!

To my children: I couldn't have written this book without you by my side encouraging and loving me through the process.

To my amazing church family who walked me through my darkness and never left my side: I love you!

To my family, especially my sister Denise: thank you for believing in and fighting for me even when I didn't have the strength to fight for myself.

table of contents

special acknowledgments

To my mom, Juanita Jordan, who went to be with the Lord on January 29th, 2018. As I was writing this book, she gave me her blessing to share our story of brokenness because she understood the power of overcoming by the blood of the Lamb and the word of our testimony.

Thank you for your example of always putting Christ first, no matter what life brought our way. I love you and can't wait to see you again so you can sing to me like you did when I was young. In those final days at hospice when I stayed with you, I'll never forget how you started to sing Amazing Grace at 3am and the beautiful little song you sang to me when I was a child. I'm sure the party's happening in heaven because you're there!

To my Uncle William and Aunt Emily Vazquez for taking me in as a young girl when I was asked to leave my home because of the rebellious state I was in. I had no idea what God had in store for me when I walked into your home. Your words, "Se puede," (you can do it) still resound in my heart. Those five years of training and love made me the woman I am today and I'm forever grateful.

introduction

The day that I walked away from it all, completely broken for the right reasons at the right time, was the best day of my life! It was the day I stepped out and the day God stepped in!

The world doesn't place much value on brokenness; after all, if it's broken, just throw it away! I grew up with a Spanish saying: "If it's garbage, it belongs in the garbage can." For many of us, the word "broken," or the idea of being broken, isn't something we display. We've been taught to keep it all together; we've been taught not to rock the boat; we've been taught not to let anyone know that we are going through a broken time or season because they would look at us as if we were crazy, weak, or just want attention. I was part of the crowd that assumed the person just wanted attention. I wanted people to "just get over it already." Brokenness is not a quality we admire in ourselves or in others.

It's so sad that even the church, a place where we are supposed to be open and vulnerable enough to receive healing, has become a place where we fake our happiness, making everyone think that we've got it all together. We walk in with our broken homes and our broken lives, but we do absolutely nothing about it. We never tell anyone because after all, what will they think of us? But truly, we will only find true freedom when we stop being concerned about what others think about us and start becoming open to the process of finding wholeness.

Brokenness is a quality that none of us should ever feel we need to run away from. Truly, when we are broken and don't care about showing it, true freedom rushes into our souls.

Allowing the process of brokenness to happen in our lives and not trying to escape it is when we are changed. Sometimes, we have to experience a breaking that leaves us no other choice but to surrender to that brokenness. The truth of the matter is that brokenness can come through different forms, one is through the hurts of others in our lives. In my case, it was my dad walking out on me, the molestation as a child and the rape as a teenager which resulted in a very rebellious young girl being asked to leave her home. Brokenness can also come through our wrong decisions and choices or disobedience to God and those who really love and care for us.

I have experienced the latter many times in my walk with God. I have also noticed in either situation, it is during these times that the hard parts of our lives began to soften in these broken places. I ran from my brokenness for years. I tried to cover it up as if to say, "I'm all good," but my life was falling apart, my marriage was falling apart, and I was trying to keep it all together. I was controlling and overbearing about trying to fix everyone else but ignored myself.

The Bible teaches that there is a time and a season for everything under heaven.[1] That includes brokenness. When I fell in love with my husband, I gave him everything. I held nothing back—I served him, I served his church, and I served our children. I truly loved God and His people, so I gave my all to everyone, but I noticed that I was constantly putting everything and everyone else above my own needs, wants, and even desires. If I wanted to go visit my friends or my family, I couldn't because we were always too busy. They weren't as important as the work I needed to do for God and His people.

The church was growing and lives were being changed. So many wonderful things were happening, so how could I be so selfish as to want time for myself? I just wanted a day to stay home from church when I wasn't feeling well or a season away from it all. Was this selfish of me? Or was it my insides yelling at me that something wasn't right, and if I didn't stop soon, I would create resentment against the man I loved.

To avoid a fight or an argument, I did nothing and said nothing. I was dying on the inside, and I had no idea what was happening.

Don't get me wrong: I believe in sacrifice and dedication. I was just afraid—afraid of expressing myself to a man who thought that everyone else's opinion was more important than mine. I thought if I said anything, it would create a war at home, or I would mess everything up that we'd worked so hard for. I even thought people would look at me as if something was wrong with me if I said "I'm done" and allowed everything to fall apart.

If I showed my brokenness, maybe we would even lose our job as pastors. After giving ourselves to this church for over eighteen years, this could have meant we would both have to start other careers. We had given it all, all our hard work, all our 401k—how would we start over? For years, I held back, not saying anything, trying to take care of everything, acting like I was God.

I had so much resentment against my husband and his decisions as a pastor. I was so broken, and no one ever knew it—not to mention all the brokenness I had to face even before we were married and the baby that died. I was a bomb about to explode.

We were buried in an unhealthy and unstable relationship, but my husband had no idea. Yes, it was through my brokenness that our lives would be restored. It was my saying "enough is enough" that saved our marriage which was going downhill super-fast. With those few words, I felt a freedom I hadn't felt in a long time. I never dreamed that brokenness would lead to this kind of freedom. I used to try to do everything under guilt and condemnation with my own efforts, instead of listening to my heart, but those days would come to an end.

I truly believe that before we can become beautiful, we need to walk through a process called brokenness. This means we need to stop pretending that everything is fine and beautiful when we know very well that there are broken areas of our lives. These must be completely surrendered to God and even to the counsel of people who really love us in order for us to be made whole. The Bible says that He is near to the broken hearted and to those who are crushed in spirit.[2]

In this book, I will walk you through some very private moments of my life where the most beautiful things have come from. I pray my story will give you courage and help you face difficult and even helpless situations in your life. Because I understand brokenness like the back of my hand, I can walk you through and let you know that you don't have to just sit there and die. You can be beautifully broken. If you give God the time He needs in your life to put the pieces back together, allowing Him to teach you, He will even show you how to put some of those pieces back together yourself.

If you get serious with God, He will get serious with you. Then you will say, just as I have said: "Truly the broken places have become the sweetest places."

chapter 1

MY BEAUTIFULLY BROKEN LIFE

If you haven't read the introduction,
please go back or you may feel a little lost.

WE RUN FROM OUR BROKENNESS,
BUT GOD RUNS TOWARDS IT.

I call my life "my beautiful broken life" because I've learned to stop being bitter over all the broken places. I have allowed God to give me beauty for the ashes.[1] This wasn't an overnight thing. Each broken experience was a process; one I thought would never end.

When my dad walked out when I was born, a void developed in my soul causing me to search for love in all the wrong places. Was it my fault he left? No, but the timing made it a challenge not to think it was. As if that wasn't bad enough, my mom became mentally ill because of the trauma of my dad deserting her. Because of her illness, she couldn't care for my sister and I, so we went to live with our grandparents whom I simply adored. Eventually, we came back to live with our mom who was in and out of mental illness episodes—not a stable home for us at all.

As a little girl, I was sexually abused by a few of mom's various boyfriends. Even though my mom was suffering with mental illness, leaving your daughters alone with boyfriends is never a good idea. I was raped at thirteen by a family member who was twenty-six. Occasionally, my mom would send us to visit our dad in Michigan. Most of the time, we stayed with our grandmother since he was usually busy with his girlfriends. When I told my dad what had happened to me, he slapped me for it. This only added to my shame and pain which drove me to act out and rebel.

Because I was unmanageable and super-rebellious from all the hurt and abuse, I was kicked out of the house at fourteen. I was so out of control. All I could remember was the black garbage bag stuffed with my clothes as I wondered why my sister got to stay but I had to leave.

My uncle begged my mom to let me live with them. She agreed and I was taken in by my aunt and uncle. I had no idea what a gift this move would be or what God had in store as a result. I was so broken that all I could think about was, "Could this family really handle me and all my mess?"

My earthly father never told me I was special or loved. I learned that from my Father God and from my uncle, yet it was still challenging for me to completely grasp a fatherly love. God's process is what helped me totally heal so I could understand my worth as a daughter of the King.

In the meantime, I ended up looking for love in wrong relationships—one boyfriend after another. I was looking for someone to fill the void in my heart. It wasn't until I gave my life to Christ that I understood, "though my father and mother forsake me, the Lord will receive me."[2] For some of you, your parents were there physically, but absent emotionally. Now, you feel emotionally bankrupt and don't understand what a privilege it is to be with you. Maybe, you're running from relationship to relationship trading one pain for another instead of waiting on your Boaz? (In the Bible, Boaz was the wonderful man who married Ruth, a widow who desired a husband.[4])

Until I asked God to come into my heart, things didn't change for me. Even after I prayed the prayer of salvation, I still needed to make certain decisions to start living a whole life. But at least now, I had God on my side to give me the strength and confidence I so desperately needed. At sixteen years of age, I had a God-encounter which marked me for the rest of my life. I would never turn away from Him even though I still made some horrible mistakes and I was hurt by people I trusted.

I had a really good friend whose husband would hit on me at church. Even though the attention would have normally lifted my ego, my empty soul didn't feel flattered since I wasn't the only one he was hitting on. His character issues gave me a distorted view of the gospel and the Bible. I soon learned that not all men are perfect and such men should step down from any kind of leadership position until they get themselves together. The Bible is filled with these kinds of stories as well as the consequences of an unrepentant heart.

Before I got married, I met a guy, and I thought he was so cute. He was Spanish, but he was light-skinned with green or blue eyes (I can't remember, LOL). We worked together, and I was so in love with him. But deep down inside, I knew he was a nice guy, but not the guy for me. I proceeded anyway even after being warned by those who loved me.

He would often buy me flowers and treated me like a queen. On my birthday I was expecting something great, but for some reason, I didn't even get a phone call. A few days later, he eventually did call me to tell me that he was at the hospital because his buddy's girlfriend was having a baby. Long story short, it was actually his baby, so he wasn't a nice guy afterall.

I was devastated! "God, why?" I cried. I was an emotional mess. I remember taking the bus to work feeling like I couldn't even walk to the bus stop. I was a senior in high school and lived in the inner city of Chicago where I grew up. On my way to work that day, I prayed and held back my tears as I pleaded with God, "Please take this pain away. I need your help." I promise you that four bus stops down the road, I felt absolutely nothing for this guy. The crazy thing about this entire story is that the pain stopped right at the corner of Fullerton and Pulaski (two cross streets in my city). Right down that same street, five years later, my husband and I would pastor a church and literally see thousands of hurting people come to Christ.

God turned my pain into purpose. Listen to me. God knows who you're ultimately supposed to spend the rest of your life with. Maybe you've been with a great guy, but he's not the guy God has for you. Just ask God to make it known to you. (Let me be clear:

> During all the disappointment, God's Word became the best love letter in my life.

I was able to pray this way because I wasn't yet married.)So many times, I'd ask myself, "Does true love even exist?" Then I would read this part of the Bible. "'For I know the plans I have for you,' declares the LORD, 'plans to prosper you and not to harm you, plans to give you hope and a future.'" [4]

time to reflect

Describe a time that you gave your heart away to the wrong person that left you hurting.

Have you forgiven them?

PRAYER

Dear God,

I give You the pain that _____ has caused in my heart. Today, I choose to forgive them and to release this unforgiveness. Take away the painful memories and give me a new start. Your Word says in Jeremiah 29:11 that You know the plans You have for me, plans to prosper me and not to harm me, plans to give me a hope and a future.[4] So today I chose to believe Your Word and expect You to do something great in my life.

In Jesus' name, Amen.

chapter 2

DOES TRUE LOVE EVEN EXIST?

HOW WE MET

I was only seventeen when I met my husband at a park during a Christian crusade. I remember before I left my house that day, I said to myself, "I need to look cute just in case I meet my husband tonight." What seventeen-year-old thinks that way? I was walking with my family, looking for somewhere to sit when I saw a familiar face. It was Danny—at least, I knew him by Danny. His real name is Daniel. I remember him because he was so cute, and he was a youth pastor—oh my goodness, what a perfect combination.

I remembered he had brought some youth to my uncle's church the previous year, but he looked different—he looked fine! The last time I saw him, he had on a Hawaiian shirt and a long beard and looked like an old man—way too old for me. This time, we talked for what seemed like hours and ended up meeting unannounced every day for five straight days, rain or shine, at the crusade in Chicago's Humboldt Park. I loved going to school and right after school, rushing home to get prepared to see him again. I always made sure I looked pretty.

When I arrived, I could sit anywhere in the midst of thousands of people because he would look for me and always find me. I loved the silent games we played. The first evening He asked me if I was seeing anyone, I told him, "No, I'm waiting on the man God has for me."

Immediately he just lifted his hands in the air and said, "Well, here I am!" I was shocked because usually that line would scare the guys off, but not this time. So, I grabbed him by the arm and began to introduce him to my family. After all, he did say, "Here I am."

Afterwards, he walked me to my car and asked me how old I was. I told him I was seventeen; I asked him how old he was. He said, "Twenty-six!" What? No way! At the time, I was living with my aunt and uncle, and I knew my uncle would not allow this relationship. My uncle's approval meant everything to me because he had taught me the importance of honoring those who love and care for you. Plus, my uncle was also my pastor. So if I wanted God's blessing over my life, I needed to make sure I honored and respected my uncle's opinion. I was so bummed because I really liked Daniel. He was so cute and loved God— what more could a girl ask for?

A TWO-YEAR WAIT. REALLY?

We talked over the phone and our feelings grew. I knew I was going to have to tell my uncle sooner or later that I was falling in love with an older guy. I finally built up the courage to tell him and just as I thought, he immediately said, "No!" So, I called up Danny and told him I wasn't allowed to talk to him anymore. He was surprised because he had never met a girl who would:

1) Get permission from her parents (guardians), and
2) Actually obey them.

This made him fall in love with me all the more because he saw something unique and different in me. Please understand this wasn't always my life style. It was a process my uncle taught me because I was so tired of being hurt in relationships. I had gotten to a point, even as a teenage girl, that I wanted to obey. I wanted God's best for my life. I was by no means a "good girl" as demonstrated by some of my very stupid decisions and mistakes, but I had just gotten to a point of complete surrender after all the hurt.

My uncle told me I needed to wait at least two years, and I obeyed. I still liked Danny, but I asked him not to come looking for me at work and not to call me. In the space of a year and a half, he called me three times just to make sure I wasn't taken— how cute was that?

I was about eighteen-and-a-half when I needed to learn some computer programs and I knew Danny worked in downtown Chicago at the school of office technology. I contacted him, but he brushed me off and forwarded my call to the correct person to help me—how rude! I called him right back and ended up showing up at his job. I was looking all pretty, of course, because I had to make a good impression. I had lunch in my hand for the two of us. I knew he wouldn't be able to resist this beautiful young girl asking for his help.

He was so happy to see me and invited me to a concert at his church he had just started to pastor. His church was named "The Fun Church," and the congregation was made up of teenagers and young adults. I was so excited; I went home to tell my uncle that I wanted to go to the concert, and he said "No!"

This time, I said, "You need to stop treating me like a little girl."

He quickly replied, "You're staying here and taking care of the kids, and I'm going." Say what? What's he thinking? What's he going to do?

He ended up going to the concert and told me absolutely nothing when he came home. Of course, I wondered what happened. My comment to my uncle, "You need to stop treating me like a little girl," must have opened his eyes. He finally gave me permission to start talking to Danny, and I was so excited. The two years of waiting was over, but I had no idea what was coming ahead.

We started to talk. Very soon, I received confirmation in my heart and in my spirit that Danny was the man for me. With all the other guys, I had felt this nasty feeling in my stomach, almost like I wanted to throw up. It was not because they were ugly—well, some of them were—but with Danny, I felt peace. When I would pray or worship, all I felt in my heart was God's approval. It was a supernatural peace. All I needed now was the approval of my uncle, and I was good to go.

I absolutely fell in love with this guy but very quickly realized I wasn't the only one who was head over heels for him. I visited his church only to be humiliated, mocked, and treated very badly by a group of girls who swore Danny was God's will for their lives. "Oh, my goodness, what is this drama?" I wondered. I would be worshiping God, and they would be right behind me, mocking me.

Can you believe I still walked in love and treated them nicely? I just knew he was my husband, and I didn't need to fight for him. Danny was very excited to have me in his life. He would take me out to dinner and we would have the time of our lives, but Danny wasn't a hundred percent sure if he wanted to marry me.

TRYING TO SEE MY VALUE

His emotions were very unstable compounded with the fact that he had other girls who liked him which his ego enjoyed. He had an emotional soul tie with one of the girls who used to mock me. I had no idea until one day in the car, he burst into tears, confessing to me his emotional confusion. I was crushed. This was very devastating to me because I had been saving myself for him.

> Sometimes the bold step needed in
> your relationship is to let go.

So eventually, I had to walk away from him. Even though it hurt, I walked away. I knew he was the man God had for me, but he didn't know it yet. I knew it wasn't my job to convince him. I let go. I had to give him a reason to chase me.

I hopped on a flight to Tulsa, Oklahoma, to Oral Roberts University to study. I knew I loved Danny and he was the only man for me for the rest of my life, but to think he wasn't sure he felt the same was extremely hurtful. I wasn't going to force him to love me back. That was the reason I left. I wanted to prove a point: I wouldn't allow him to mess with my feelings, and I would give him an opportunity to really think about what he wanted in life.

I was finally beginning to know who I was and my worth because my uncle had poured his love into me. I was special, valuable and tough although I didn't fully understand it overnight or for many years to come. I wanted God to change me by helping me see myself the way He saw me.

The next few months in Oklahoma were so hard. My hurting heart was making it difficult to focus on school and God. I was lovesick. I kept strong, with very little communication on my end, until Danny couldn't take it anymore. Finally, I felt a ray of hope—he came to Tulsa to get me and we got engaged.

When I returned home, I was surprised to discover that Danny wasn't fully over the woman he had a soul tie with. Because of my experiences with my dad walking away from me, I couldn't handle even a hint of wondering if Danny, the man I thought I was going to spend the rest of my life with, wasn't sure of what he wanted. Once, I remember being so upset at a family meeting that I was crying. In front of everyone, I told Danny, "My dad walked out. Now, you're going to walk out."

My uncle got so upset at me. He said, "You don't ever do that—crying like a baby over a man. You can cry, but not in front of him. He doesn't even know what he wants, so he hasn't earned the privilege of seeing you cry right now."

I hadn't learned the value of saving my full scope of emotions for the person who is fully committed to me. I was in love and I gave my entire heart to this man who would share all my life experiences. I did not understand that it should be a gradual process. I thought that because he was my fiancé, he had the right to know all my emotions. However, because he was unsure, my uncle was helping me see that Danny didn't have the honor or privilege of having all my heart until he was fully committed to me. I'm so thankful for that insight and perspective on my value and worth.

With this new revelation, I approached the situation with Danny in a whole new way. I could see the pain he was in and how he wanted freedom from his confusion and divided heart. Compassion for him filled my soul because I knew he was the one, and the love of Christ overtook my heart at that moment. I prayed for that soul tie to be broken, and it was.

A VISION OF HOPE

With Danny's heart clear and focused and my heart bursting with love, we got married. His church, my church, and his pastor's church all gathered for our wedding with close to five hundred people in attendance. It was the happiest day of my life: February 18, 1995. The wedding was outside and the weather was beautiful and sunny—what a blessed day!

Because of my parent's fractured relationship, I never really understood what a vision for a happy marriage looked like. I had never seen my mom married, so I didn't understand what it would or should look like. I'm so thankful for my uncle and aunt who took me in at fourteen in the midst of my rebellion. I was able to see and experience what a healthy strong marriage looked like for five years. Without this role model, I believe it would have been very difficult for me to navigate and understand what a healthy marriage was or could be.

I would encourage you to surround yourself with healthy married couples who can model a good marriage to you. This will give you hope and a vision for your own marriage. Believe me, they're out there! Ask the Holy Spirit to show you.

NOT PERFECT, BUT WORTH IT

That first evening of our honeymoon, my husband broke the news to me that his mom would be living with us. I thought, "OK, she does seem like a very quiet lady, and she works twelve hours a day." She was always on my side, even before we got married. She would hang up the phone on any other girls that would call Danny when we were dating, and she would always tell them that he was with me. She called me "the girl that laughs a lot." Once she told Danny, "You know that girl that laughs a lot? Well, she's going to be your wife." Now, when your mom tells you something like that, you better listen. Plus, his mom wasn't just any woman—she was a God-fearing, prayer warrior kind of mama. So, she would set him straight.

She lived with us for eight months and gave me the love and guidance that I so desperately needed from an older woman. Sometimes, we can push off the greatest blessings in our lives— our mothers-in-law—because of selfishness. At first, I was selfish because I believed that a married couple should leave the family to cleave to each other. However, as I read God's Word, I noticed that the first year of marriage was actually a time that the family, especially the girl's side of the family, would take in the married couple for the first year to help them. This was so needed in my life, and my mother-in-law fulfilled my need for a listening ear and godly counsel. Had this not been the case, my mother-in-law could have caused a wedge in our marriage, but this was never the case. She was a blessing from God.

Our marriage has experienced the good, the bad, and the very ugly. What I want you to see is that through it all, the broken places truly did become the sweetest places. So, if you're ready and willing, hang on tight, because all the brokenness you've faced doesn't have to be the end—it can be the beginning of something beautiful.

time to reflect

What healthy married couples do you surround yourself with that model a good marriage to you, even if you're not married?

What are some of the things you've observed that you want to incorporate into your life and marriage?

PRAYER

Lord Jesus,

Help me surround myself with the right people that will pour hope into my future relationships. Your Word says in Proverbs that if I walk with the wise, I will become wise, but a companion of fools suffers harm.[1] So I ask You, Holy Spirit, to lead me to the right couple or couples that would be a reflection of You in my life and remove all the fools that pull me away from You.

In Jesus' name, Amen.

chapter 3

NO, NOT MY BABY!

DID I NOT HAVE ENOUGH FAITH?

We waited four years to have a baby because we wanted to travel and focus on the ministry God had called us to. After four years, I became pregnant with our first baby. I was so excited. I loved my life and looked forward to possibly quitting my job. I was an office manager for a financial company in downtown Chicago. Now, I'd possibly be staying home. Even though it might be financially tight, we were willing to make the sacrifice. I was almost eight months pregnant when I woke up one Saturday morning. My normally very active baby was not moving.

I called out to Danny and asked him to bring me some orange juice because that would always make the baby move around, but nothing—no movement at all. I was so scared. We rushed to Northwestern Hospital in downtown Chicago about ten to fifteen minutes away. It was November and the holidays were right around the corner. I was looking forward to holding my baby in my arms. This wasn't supposed to be happening.

The doctors rushed in to do the ultrasound and all kinds of tests but soon stopped. They gave us the crushing news that our baby had died. My first reaction was to turn to my husband and believe God for our baby to come back to life. That miracle didn't come. Instead, I delivered a lifeless baby boy. I'd already been through so much pain in my life, and now this. How could this be?

> I am not ashamed to say I will believe God, even when faced with death. And I believe that's when our faith graduates—when we're willing to believe God, even if we don't get what we thought we would.

DOES IT EVER STOP?

The enemy reminded me of every horrible incident in my life and played that recording repeatedly in my head. I had to break free from his lies that the rest of my life would be horrible as well. I refused to live there, and you've got to refuse to live there, too.

I would be depressed for a few days, and then I'd get so mad at the enemy that I'd put my worship music on. Then, all his accusations and lies would have no other choice but to stop. I was learning how desperately I needed God and how I couldn't afford to go extended periods of times without praying, worshiping, or reading my Bible.

A WORSHIPER WAS BIRTHED

I couldn't handle the pain of losing a child, so we went to Florida to be prayed over and cared for by my husband's pastors. I was crushed, devastated, and very confused about my relationship with God. I would wake up and go to sleep with so much pain in my aching heart. I didn't hear God say anything to me and I wasn't saying anything to Him either.

I didn't shower. I didn't want to eat. I was so depressed. After a few days, I jumped into the shower. With milk coming out of my breasts yet no baby to feed, I raised my hands, and cried, "God, I don't understand, but I trust you. God, I don't understand, but I'll worship you anyway."

> When I stayed quiet, I was dying inside. But when I opened my mouth and started to worship God, I felt this broken place in my life become a sweet place.

When I gave in to God, a peace came upon my life instantly. All the pain, agony, and sorrow disappeared like smoke vanishing in the air. The pain that I felt no longer gripped my soul, and I found myself in tears, worshipping God, the God I loved and trusted. This time I wasn't questioning Him because I was too busy worshiping Him. Even though my baby had gone to heaven way too soon, a worshiper was birthed inside of me.

The enormous amount of peace that filled my life was so overwhelming that I didn't want to leave that bathroom shower. I've always loved to worship God, but this was different because I was worshipping within the broken place of my life. There's nothing like going through hell and still lifting your hands in trust and worship to God. It almost sounds weird—why would I worship when I'm broken? I didn't have all the answers; I just knew that I never wanted to leave that beautiful place of worship. Had I never gone through this brokenness, I would have never found that glorious presence of His peace.

Worship is therapy—it's the therapy of the Almighty. We may go to counselors and therapy sessions and that's all fine and dandy. But I'll tell you right now—there's no therapy like God's therapy, and it's found in worship! You must worship your way through brokenness. For the first time in my life, I learned to worship God in my broken place.

The next time you face devastation, I want you to turn on some worship music, lift your hands in the air and say, "God, I don't understand, but I will worship you. God, I don't understand, but I will trust you."

I came back to my home church and allowed my pain to show. I wanted our church to understand what they should do when they face devastation. I still cried and I still hurt, but every time I did, I raised my hands to worship God, telling Him how much I loved and trusted Him.

I ended up building a choir within that year. Giving myself over to God and teaching others what to do during brokenness gave me the strength to overcome this painful season of my life. I literally was putting my pain on display through worship.

OVERCOMING FEAR

The doctors said I should give myself three months to heal before attempting to get pregnant again. Three months felt like forever. I had to battle depression and all the hormonal changes from the birth of the baby we lost. The only thing that kept me sane was my worship to God. I had music playing 24/7 in my home and in my car. I finally became pregnant right at the third month, and we were so excited.

The thought popped in my head to wait a few months before we told anyone just in case something happened. But my husband and I agreed, "No! We won't walk in fear!" We chose to immediately tell all our friends and family members. Fear would try to grip my soul, especially as I was getting bigger. I had to fight the enemy's lies, "What if you lose this baby, too?"

I became this wild lady on a mission to silence that voice. I sat myself down on the living room floor with my Bible and spoke God's Word to my unborn child. I quoted scriptures over my tummy and my baby saying, "You are fearfully and wonderfully made."[1] I declared this word over my baby and commanded the fear to leave, in Jesus' name. I would proclaim, "You will live and not die and declare the works of the Lord."[2] I overcame fear with the Word of God.

The following November, I gave birth to Faith Diamond Cruz, our sweet little baby girl. After that, they just kept popping out of me. We now have two biological boys and two girls, and an adopted older daughter making a total of five wonderful children—true gifts from God.

A few years ago, my girlfriend's beautiful eleven-year-old daughter suddenly died. She had a virus of some kind. After taking a medication prescribed for her, she started to foam at the mouth and died in her mother's arms. This was so difficult for my friend especially since her husband had passed away two years before that. I had no words to say. All I could do was to comfort her and walk with her through her brokenness.

No one understood why she had to go through this pain of losing her husband and her daughter. As a church, we supported her financially and emotionally. It was very challenging for me to see my girlfriend in this kind of condition. Sometimes you don't have the words to say and that's okay. Hurting people just need for us to walk them through their brokenness, even if we just silently sit with them.

A few years later, my friend was helping out at the church. My husband and I remembered a good friend named Felix who faithfully served at my uncle's church. He never really had a girlfriend; we just knew him as the nicest guy alive. So, we introduced my friend to him. Felix joined her in a church project that we arranged for them to get to know each other. Occasionally, my husband and I have played the game of connecting people together; it's been lots of fun.

Within a year, they ended up getting married. Felix became the man she needed in her life. Out of her own mouth, she told me horrible stories about what her first husband had put her through. Having Felix in her life was a dream come true. The Lord used Felix to heal her broken places. If she had thought her life was over when her husband and daughter had passed away and made a stupid decision like ending her own life, she would have never experienced this healing love and support from Felix.

Guess what? A few years into their marriage, she got pregnant. Doctors had told her that she'd never have a baby again. She not only got pregnant, she ended up having twins—a boy and a girl. They are now enjoying their new family and love together. I could just shout right now at the goodness God showered over this family.

The broken places can become the sweetest places. Don't despise life's difficult times, because something good is getting ready to come out of it. If you learn to respond the correct way, God will turn it around. This family responded by trusting in the midst of the pain. Amid all the tears and confusion, God came through for them in a powerful way.

time to reflect

What are some of the painful things the enemy reminds you of and plays repeatedly in your head?

What worship music do you enjoy that helps you focus on the hope you have in God? Play it!

PRAYER

Father,

Today, I take up the authority I have as Your child and I command the enemy to be silent. God, forgive me of my sin and any decisions that have been an open door for the enemy to torment me in this way. I want to live my life for You and close the door to sin and disobedience in my life so I can use my authority with conviction and power. Now Satan, in the name of Jesus, I command You to leave my heart and mind right now. I give You no more rights or permission. God has great things in store for me. My future is blessed and I can laugh at tomorrow because I know that God's already there.

In Jesus' name, Amen.

> *Strength and dignity are her clothing and she laughs at the time to come.* —*Proverbs 31:25*

chapter 4

LOVING THE MAN I HATE

HOW DID I GET TO THIS PLACE?

I lived my life for God, my husband, and my children, but I didn't realize I was slowly growing cold towards the man I adored. This wasn't an overnight change. One day, I felt I had experienced enough and I told my husband I was leaving him and the church. My husband was the lead pastor of our church and the overseer of a few other churches we had planted, so this decision was going to radically change everything.

For years, I failed at trying to get his attention to understand my frustrations and feelings of neglect. It seemed there was no attempt to meet any of my needs. My fear of his disapproval and uncontrollable anger kept me silent for fear of disrupting the peace in our home for the sake of our children. Rocking the boat wasn't an option for me.

> "How much longer can this woman take being with me?
> If I were her, I would leave myself."

Danny would secretly say this to himself. He didn't see it right away but he was doing what he saw his dad do. Danny verbally abused me for years and I thought nothing of it. I thought "abuse" meant physical abuse or cheating on your spouse. I didn't even recognize verbal abuse was included in the "abuse category" for years.

I used to be so afraid of getting into the car after church because I knew that he would get on my case about something. He would yell at me because I did the wrong thing, I said the wrong thing, or I hurt someone's feelings. He would accuse me of things that weren't even true without asking about my side of the story. This behavior went on for years.

He would take everyone's side at church and leave me defenseless and emotionally abandoned. He used to call me "Jezebel" (the name of a powerfully deceptive, manipulative woman in the Bible). When I would see happy marriages, I would think to myself, "That's impossible," even after seeing a good role model in my uncle and aunt.

I would cry and endure his words rather than stand up for myself. I had a damaged mindset believing that I should stay because it was the "right thing to do." I felt like my marriage had to be an example to our church and pleasing to God. Our relationship was definitely not in the best state for us at all. God wasn't at the center of our marriage or either of our lives and it was time for that to change.

Finally, after having enough, I stood up for myself and walked away from the verbal abuse after eighteen years. Had I known any better, I would have done it sooner. Walking out for those three months was the first stand I took for myself and, ultimately, our marriage. I understood my worth and what God thought about me, and this wasn't it.

If we choose to live in fear, we stay in the abuse. I questioned, "How am I going to make it?" I wanted to be a lawyer when I was in college, but when I heard God clearly say to me, "I've called you to ministry," I went to Bible school instead. So there I was, my life and family falling apart all because I refused that mess.

God began to comfort me. I went to my husband's pastor's church in Florida to spend a week away from it all. They believed God for my marriage. I told them, "Don't believe for my marriage cause it ain't going to happen." I was so done!

I was at the altar at their church, enjoying God's presence, enjoying my freedom from that verbal mess, and enjoying being away. I was crying when God began to speak to me. He said "I'm still going to use you for My glory."

I was so excited that the pastors mistakenly thought God had told me to go back to my husband. I said, "Nope, God told me that He's still going to use me!" They still rejoiced with me. Actually, the pastor's wife was laughing. She was probably cheering me on inside because she has a story of her own to tell.

She would laugh and say, "Oh my goodness, Jennifer." God wasn't telling me anything bad about myself, I was used to hearing that from my husband. Instead, He was telling me how much He loved me. I love that about God. He's not only a wonderful Father but He's a good friend.

One day, my husband came to Florida to see me. I was very upset because I needed space, not him trying to smother me with meaningless words. He arrived with a little popcorn bag from my favorite shop. I said, "Danny, I don't need your popcorn. What I need is my needs placed above any others and not be treated the way I have been for so long." I knew I was a good wife. I felt I was the glue that had kept our family together. Maybe that was unhealthy, but I knew no other way.

We had our beautiful children and a successful ministry, so a breakdown wasn't part of the picture or our plan. I was always trying to put on the happy face to cover up for what was really happening until I just got tired of it all. I was trying to be God, always trying to fix everything to cover up for him. God had to bring me to a place of complete brokenness. If it meant starting my life over again, then I was willing.

Finally, I was done. I reached my breaking point. Even though Danny held my arm asking me not to do this, I walked out with our baby in the other arm. The years of neglect, not considering my opinion, and not prioritizing our goals as a family were done. The years of getting into the car after church to argue over something stupid were over. I was tired of holding up the mask to my face every Sunday.

I did things to validate my own worth, but they were always related to my performance. My worth started to come from what others perceived of me therefore I felt the need to constantly demonstrate how great I was. My desire was to always look good while being miserable and exhausted inside. Both my husband and I seriously needed soul surgery and it would only come from humbling ourselves before God.

What I needed most was for God to deal with my identity.

Even though I wanted to allow others to have access to my life, I felt I couldn't because I was a pastor's wife. We had an image to maintain and the unspoken rule was to always "protect" or cover my husband. "Never show your less than fabulous feelings; never talk back; obey all the time; don't fight; and don't make a mistake"—this was the recording that played in my head over and over until I couldn't take it any longer.

I saw the anger rising in his face and in his tone. "Are you crazy, Jen, what are you thinking? You're just going to throw it all away?" (This collapse happened in October of 2012, the same year I won the title of Mrs. Illinois. It felt like the worst year of my life—yet, was it?)

I finally did it. I walked away from my husband and our church after eighteen years of marriage and ministry dedication. I grabbed our children and went to live with my sister and her family for a few months. I finally felt free, and even though I knew I would lose it all, I didn't care. I felt free from obligations, free to visit my family, free from being forced to go to church when I wasn't feeling well (which wasn't often). I was free to say what I pleased and what I felt. I was not going to be under his control or anger any more.

I didn't even want to see my husband's face. He had never cheated on me or raised a finger to hit me. I was just done. I had no love for him at all. When he would come to visit me at my sister's house, I would get on his case about trivial things like not taking his shoes off when he walked into the house. These selfish acts and not considering the value or requests of others bothered me before, but by this time I was ready and able to say and do something about it.

If I didn't do something right or to his liking, he was very harsh with me. It stunk being in my shoes, but I put on the happy face for the happy pictures and the crown of Mrs. Illinois. In the past, I would ask for marriage counseling but he wasn't willing. He would always put on a happy face in front of his pastor. But by this time, I would blast him. I was tired of defending him and picking up the slack. I was way past being done. I remember telling God, "If you called Faithworld Church into existence, You're going to have to be God enough to keep Faithworld Church going."

time to reflect

Describe a time in your life that you felt like breaking down. Have you spoken to someone like a pastor or an elder at your church? Finding someone that you can trust who can give you godly counsel is so important.

PRAYER

Father,

I present this breakdown I'm feeling to You. Your Word says in 1 Peter[1] to cast my care upon You because You care for me. Today I ask You for a godly person, preferably a pastor or church leader, to show me Your wisdom so I can make the correct decisions in my life. I'll submit myself to their advice and maintain a teachable heart.

In Jesus' name I pray, Amen.

chapter 5

A VOICE IN THE WILDERNESS

THE DAY GOD TEXTED ME

I was in such a desperate situation. I needed to hear from God or I would never return to my husband again. I was in my bathroom where I spent so many days just depressed over my life and wondering if I had made the right decision. All of the sudden, I received a text message from none other than Marilyn Hickey.

"Why in the world was Marilyn Hickey texting me?" I thought. I never asked to be a part of her mailing or texting list. I called her ministry and I asked them, "How did I get on her texting list?"

And they responded, "I don't know, ma'am. Even if we wanted to, that's not something we offer any longer."

For six months, I received texts from "Marilyn Hickey" telling me exactly what I needed to do. She was basically a stranger to me and had no idea what my specific situation was to begin with. When I was sixteen years old, my uncle received a magazine at the house from this "Marilyn Hickey lady". As I looked through its pages, I saw how powerfully God used her. I told my uncle, "I want to be just like her."

And he said, "Absolutely, you can." In this dark hour of my life, the Holy Spirit reminded me of those very words.

Through the prayers of my husband and our church members, I finally reached the point where I began to pray, "God, I want Your perfect will for my life, not Your permissive will for my life." Before then, I was bent on doing my own thing which meant I would have totally missed out on my destiny and the lives I was meant to touch.

I had to fight this battle and overcome so that my children and spiritual children could overcome as well! This "text" thing was so supernatural. God orchestrated events out of my control. He arranged these text messages from this amazing woman who loved and served God with her whole being. This let the devil know that God's voice overpowered him and spoke louder—so loud that he had no choice but to shut up.

God stepped in through technology. I felt like all of heaven was fighting for me when I couldn't fight for myself. God stepped into the ring. I was on my bathroom floor when I received that first text and I just cried out. God proved to me that when man walks out, He walks in. Never forget that.

Text Number One:

> *"Be careful whose advice you take, even from family because Absalom's mom gave him advice that destroyed him even to death."*

At that time, I was determined to get a divorce and had certain family members pressing me to do so as well.

Text Number Two:

> *"Guard your heart from rebellion. The devil will use rebellion and has you in a trance while you lose everything that God has given you."*

I was in such a rebellious state because of all the hurt. Had I not turned from it quickly, I would have lost everything that God had given me. I still couldn't believe how God was texting me through Marilyn Hickey, helping me to get back on my feet again. I am forever grateful that she hears his voice and did exactly what he asked of her. I look forward to sharing this story with her.

(There were more text messages and stories and I will share later in my next book.)

DOING IT MY WAY

I wept like a baby. How did she know what to say? God made Himself so real to me even though I still felt trapped—trapped in anger, in hurt, and in confusion. I cried after every text message. I felt as though the enemy wanted to ask God if he could kill me, and God responded, "NO."

Even though he couldn't kill me, the enemy still had access to me because of the pride which was such a huge part of my life. This was one of the main reasons I needed to go through this process of removing all of the parts of me that weren't God designed.

I had no idea my pride was destroying my life and my relationships. I finally recognized how ugly my heart really was, but I also started to see a ray of hope. I knew I no longer wanted a divorce. It wasn't until I was open and honest with God that I felt chains start to fall off of me.

> I went from wanting a divorce to crying out to God for his perfect will in my life.

I never wanted to live my life outside of God's perfect will. That was too scary a thought for me. I knew the difference and I had experienced so much damage in life already that living outside of His will wasn't an option. But my pride and rebellion almost stole that principle from me. Hanging out with the wrong people and listening to the wrong advice almost ruined my life, but God stepped in when I cried out.

time to reflect

Describe a situation in your life that God made Himself so real to you.

These times are so important to write down and remember. Anytime the enemy starts to question your God and the things He has done for you, you need to be able to point back to a victory, even if it's super small. Don't allow pride to say, "God's never done anything for me." If you're alive and reading this, then you know He has given you life. Dig deep through the vault of your heart and celebrate those precious events.

PRAYER

Lord Jesus,

I give You my heart. I surrender my life completely to You, Father. I want to live in the plan and purpose You have for me. Reveal Yourself to me and open the eyes of my heart to see all the wonderful things You're doing and are about to do in my life.

In Jesus' name, Amen.

"Give thanks in all circumstances; for this is God's will for you in Christ Jesus." 1 Thessalonians 5:18

chapter 6

FINDING MY WAY BACK HOME

One of my main problems—I thought I was God and needed to fix everything or it would all fall apart. Even though we were building a great ministry in the city of Chicago with thousands of people being impacted and churches being birthed, it was being done in such an unhealthy way that it all came crashing down. I'm so grateful it did. I needed to reach the end of me, the end of living this way. It was so exhausting. I needed an end to it all so I could experience a new beginning. It was challenging at the time because I couldn't see this new start, but I cherish the length God went to, to prove Himself so real to me.

> God taught me a valuable lesson—that He was God,
> and I wasn't.

My sister Denise and her husband Carlos loved me back to life and biblically confronted my husband, helping him understand that if he ever wanted me back, there would need to be major changes in his life. I got upset with my sister and brother-in-law at one point because I told them, "I'm done. Why are you giving him hope?" They knew better and simply did not respond to me. They just continued to love me and the children.

We had so much fun even though I was so broken at this time. My sister and I restored our relationship. Many times, we laughed and cried together into the wee hours of the morning even if she had to go to work the next day. This experience was very humbling because I had always been so judgmental of my sister for stupid reasons. Yet God in His mercy and infinite wisdom used my sister and her husband to restore me back to life.

Sometimes, we don't realize how ugly we are on the inside. When we start criticizing other people who don't live the way we think they should, God will allow us to get to a place of brokenness so we can be humbled and understand how much we ourselves are just as much in need of a Savior.

A few months later, we returned home even though I still felt no love for my husband. He decorated our entire home and prepared it so beautifully for Christmas, something he hadn't done in a long time. I still didn't care. I was in a zone and didn't allow him access. It wasn't until he and the church started to fast that I felt something happen. The church we laid down our lives for was now laying down their lives for us.

The fast started a few days before New Year's Eve 2012. My husband fasted for forty days. While I was living at my sister's house, he took the only thing I left in my closet—a white dress I used to preach in. He put it on my side of our bed and started to declare that I would come back and sleep there.

On New Year's Eve, I decided to allow him to come with me to my uncle's church since that was where I was going during our separation. I agreed to return home under one condition—that he would sleep in the basement, and I would sleep in our bedroom alone. He agreed because he was just happy to get me home.

As I slept in our bed, I still didn't love him, not even one ounce, not even an inch—nothing. He would ask me, "Do you love me?" And I would say, "No, not even one percent—nothing." During this time, I was the principal of the school at our church. What was supposed to be a joint venture was left in my lap. I had the total responsibility to run the entire school due to the lack of my husband's involvement. This caused me to despise him. I wouldn't have even started the school to begin with had I known I would have to shoulder so much responsibility on my own. So often, this was my pattern—to say "yes" even if it was to my own detriment.

THE BASEMENT BEDROOM

There was a couple in our church, Jonathan and Julia, who came to our home. Without saying a word, Jonathan helped my husband move all his things to the basement. Julia helped me get situated in our bedroom upstairs. They did it all with such a loving heart. I'm so thankful for non-judgmental church people like Jonathan and Julia and another loving couple, Rich and Betsy. We had a lot to learn from them. How they walked us through brokenness with such understanding was a testimony of God's love for us.

I remember saying to them, "I guess you're experiencing and seeing the death of a situation. It's because you'll also see a resurrection." I still felt compelled to speak hope to them regarding our marriage, but after I said that, I thought, "What did I just say?" They didn't judge our situation, they walked us through it. I am sure they were simply happy to see me come back home to at least try. They still faithfully serve at our church today.

> The Church would be so much healthier if we Christians could simply love people in the middle of their mess—even if it's our pastor.

Loving and agreeing with someone's plight are two different things, so don't confuse them. I'm thankful for all the godly confrontations I received. I'm thankful for those who spoke up to share their hearts with me. And I'm so grateful they gave me room to be me, to be hurt, mad and upset. Some may walk away because of your honesty and that's okay. Perhaps they weren't meant to walk with you anyway.

During this time, I completely stepped out of ministry because I understood I was in no position to serve. My reserves were depleted and I couldn't help anyone because I had nothing to draw upon. I was just not able or willing to position myself as a "fake" in front of God's people anymore. I'd already done it for too long. I stood before the church and let them know I needed a time of healing and restoration. My pain was so deep from eighteen years of living a cover story.

We would bump into each other as we walked through our home as if we were strangers. Our children felt the separation and distance with him in the basement and me in our bedroom. But soon, God started dealing with my life. I would hear my husband's prayers from the basement through the vents. They upset me so much, I tried to close the vents to block the sound. I said to myself, "Why is he praying? I'm not going back to him."

I believe in my heart that because we had relentless church families in Indiana and Chicago praying and fasting, I began to feel a shift in my heart. I remember one day feeling a little something in my heart, like a tiny ounce of love. a tiny pinch or spark and wondered what it was. I tried to ignore it, but I couldn't.

THE CHILDREN DANCED

That day, I actually sat down with him at the kitchen table. Up until then I wouldn't go anywhere near him or even allow him to talk to me, but this day I simply sat at the kitchen table. Our children saw this and all four children under the age of twelve danced together. They started dancing like I'd never seen them dance before. I was crushed to think about the pain, the silent pain they had been facing. I had neglected their needs.

One little glimpse of hope set their souls on fire that evening. I went down to the basement and knocked on his door and asked him if I could come in. He was surprised—shocked—all of the above. He said, "Yes, of course." I slept in the basement bedroom that evening with him, and all I could say was that I felt better.

Danny asked me, "How much do you love me?"

I said, "Ten percent."

A few weeks later, he asked me again, "How much do you love me?"

I said, "Twenty-five percent." He was so happy I was growing in love with him. God began dialing up the love and the passion I had for my husband. It wasn't all that hard once He really began to work.

But God created the first spark.

Danny would take whatever I would give him; he was just happy I loved him again. He worked hard at winning my love. He would bring me tea and cookies almost every night.

There was a war being waged against our marriage and the enemy was trying to keep us apart. Even though things were improving, I was still in such a deep depression over all the events that had transpired the past few months. I could hear the voice of the enemy screaming in my ear, "Your life is over. Your ministry is over. Your family is over." Every morning, I woke up with his voice in my ear and a migraine headache.

Practically speaking, Danny still had to work at the church and put food on our table. By this time, he had been away three months and the church lost many people. People who I thought loved us walked away leaving behind lies and assumptions. We received letters and emails filled with lies about us and the ministry. We were so crushed to think that the people we laid our lives down for would kick us when we were down.

In the morning, Danny would go to work and come back to find me in the same place he left me on the bathroom floor, depressed and wondering if I really wanted to fight for it all. I literally had no strength. When I think about the process of all of this, it makes me cry because of how much I love my husband now. I can't believe we went through all that brokenness. It was much needed but the work wasn't done yet.

One Sunday, I was at my uncle's church when the music ministry team started to sing a song called "Break Every Chain."[1] As they sang, I felt God begin to break every chain off my life. God did it, not me. He broke the chains of pride, fear, and rebellion when

I surrendered. And in that moment, I felt the winds of change blowing my way.

CHANGE IS GOOD

The days of my sitting on my bathroom floor, depressed and unsure of life were over. Suddenly, I started to experience more and more freedom with every text message, prayer, fast, tear and prayer of surrender. God started showing me where I was wrong and what I could do to change me. Every time I cried out to God over the ugly person I had allowed myself to become, I felt layer after layer being peeled off of me.

Broken can become beautiful. God can make the sweetest places form right out of our brokenness. I no longer walked around with heaviness over me. That heaviness was literally making me look old and in need of plastic surgery, Botox or something. Once it lifted, it felt like God gave me a face lift, and the best part was it was free. Well mostly free. Actually, it did cost me a lot of tears, but I'm so glad that I followed God on this journey to wholeness in Him.

You know what turned my husband back to me? Putting my foot down and letting him know I'm not playing games. It should be a privilege to be with you, not an obligation. Don't try to force anyone to stay with you. I'm sure you have areas in need of improvement like I did and still do but it's important to acknowledge your strengths.

If you look at Proverbs 31, the woman spoken of here had a number of great qualities. As a matter of fact, the Bible says her husband "praises her."[2] You may ask, "How can we get to that point?" Here are a few places to start:

- Recognize who you are in Christ.
- Allow God to work on your worth and value.
- Give God your insecurities, failures, let downs, hurts, and mistakes and start walking with your head up high. (We don't do these things full of pride, but in the secure knowledge of who we are, knowing that we are priceless and beautiful before God.)
- Don't allow anyone to beat you up, either verbally or physically.
- See yourself as God sees you.

For years I didn't need a man; what I needed was for God to work on my bad, hurtful attitude that would have scared every man away.

If you have a mouth problem, you shouldn't be praying for a man. You should be praying for and working on your mouth. I know this is strong advice, but we don't realize we have the power to build up or to destroy our own home. We can easily destroy it with our big mouths.

Once you have worked on the areas that are yours to deal with, acknowledge it is a privilege to be with you. This isn't a prideful statement; it's understanding your worth and your value in Christ. Women who don't understand this often go for the first bozo they find instead of waiting for their Boaz.

FREEDOM REQUIRES BOLDNESS

The catch is that many of us won't be bold enough to walk out of the abuse. Many times, we are in this kind of situation because we've given a man something that only belongs to God. We give what belongs to God to our friends, our kids, and a man, and then we don't know how to pick ourselves up when they abandon us or hurt us.

> There's a portion of your heart
> that belongs to no one but God.

One lady's husband left her for another woman. She ended up in the hospital because she tried to kill herself. She forgot about her babies that needed her and about her future that could be much brighter had she let that man out of her heart. I was so angry when I heard this—I wanted to go breathe some sense into her and help her see everything she had to live for and set her free from feeling her life was over without him.

Sometimes, we don't know how to walk away from the abuse when leaving, even if it is only for a season, is the best thing we could do. I'm so glad I did because my man is a better man and our marriage is better than it's ever been.

We look for our guys to fill all the needs of our hearts, and when they don't, we freak out—this is our biggest problem. I love my husband to tell me I'm beautiful and the best thing that has ever happened to him, but if he doesn't do it all the time, I'm not falling apart. I know how to get on my face, and my father God tells me I'm beautiful every day.

Stop looking for a man to validate you. If you're feeling that way, it's because you've given that portion of your heart away to a human relationship. It's only in God's presence in worship and in prayer that this portion of the heart can truly be satisfied. My husband turned into a man madly in love with me. He now treats me like I'm the only women alive. Even now that we are back together, we still don't give God's portion of our hearts to each other. We understand and honor the fact that we are not able to meet all of each other's needs.

When God started to break my husband, he knew he didn't have to tell me anything because God was dealing with my heart as well. God wasn't pushing me, but at the right time, God made it happen. My husband had key men speak into his life knowing I wasn't coming back unless he chose to change.

He was so determined that he fasted for forty days and grew very skinny, but he knew that if God didn't come through for him, our relationship would be over. Sure enough, I started to feel something shift in my heart because of a praying man—a man who left preaching at the altar and returned to praying at the altar for me. That says a lot about my husband as a preacher; he's a true man. I came back home to him and I love him.

time to reflect

Have you ever thought about the idea of "a portion of your heart belonging to God alone and never to another person?" How would things be different if you put this into action in your own life?

PRAYER

Father,

Today I'm reserving a portion of my heart for You and You alone. It doesn't belong to my spouse, the love of my life, a family member or my best friend. That portion belongs to You alone. Help me to always remember this.

In Jesus' name, Amen.

"Love the Lord your God with all your heart all your soul and with all your mind." –Matthew 22:37

chapter 7

GOD WANTED TO MEND MORE RELATIONSHIPS

MY MOM

Hating someone is such a strong and exhausting emotion. I held on to so much hate in my heart towards certain individuals but one that hurt deeply was my own mother. As a child, I didn't understand her mental condition, so all of her negative and destructive choices hurt me to the core. I distanced myself from her for many years and it wasn't until I gave my life to Christ that I was able to come to a starting point of forgiveness and understanding. Even then, our relationship was so bruised.

My mom didn't understand how to once again parent a teenage girl who was devastated from being asked to leave her home on top of the other violations I experienced. For many years, I just called her and served her because I thought it was the right thing to do. It wasn't until she was diagnosed with stage four cancer and didn't really have the strength to argue with me that we were able to work on a meaningful relationship.

Those final two years were so precious to me. It's like God was allowing us to make up for lost time. I so enjoyed serving my mom and staying over at hospice with her. During that time, she gave me permission to share our story with the world. This was so important to me because I never wanted to dishonor her.

A week before she passed, the first thing she did when I walked into her hospice room was to show me her hands as if to say, "Why haven't you done my nails?" So, my hubby went to buy her some nails and I lovingly put them on, cherishing every moment. That was the last day we had a semi-understandable conversation. I have heard so many other people's stories and experiences with my mom since then which were a blessing. Some made me crack up. For example, someone took Mom to get groceries at Aldi's and she came down ready to go in her fancy fur coat, a little over the top for groceries. In hospice, they sang this song called "The Juanita Song" that melted my hard heart towards my mom:

> "Juanita, you are beautiful,
> Juanita, you are strong.
> Unique and precious woman,
> You've been perfect all along.
> Juanita, hear our love song."

I broke and cried like a baby over the silent judgement I held in my heart. Listen, it doesn't matter what our parents did or didn't do for us. Today is a good day to forgive and not take that bitterness into tomorrow because you are only harming yourself. Your parents gave you what they had and what they knew, so let it go. If they were emotionally bankrupt, they couldn't give you the love and support which you needed. It's time to understand that and show compassion. Be the bigger person and show them the love they never received.

The last two years with my mom were our best times together. She was so understanding when it came to my role in ministry. If I had something happening, she would always tell me to take care of God's house—His people. She understood and respected God's call on my life. If she had something she needed me to do, she would tell me, "We can take care of that tomorrow, but you're not missing church."

Church and ministry were a priority to her and she made sure I understood that. She gave me the affirmation I needed as a pastor. She would tell me, "Not everyone will understand your lifestyle, but this is what God has called you to do." I'll never forget that example. I love you, Mom. This broken place has become a sweet place in our relationship. She's now at peace in heaven and I'm at peace on earth.

BACKSTABBING FRIENDS

My husband and I have loved deeply and poured our lives into certain friendships and relationships, but at our weakest moments, several took advantage of us by spreading lies. My husband was so devastated. He was fighting to save his marriage all the while having to deal with outrageously false accusations.

We couldn't take it anymore. Danny decided to give it to God, yet I felt I had to say something about it. I was done holding back my true feelings so I called each of these people on the phone. I didn't curse, yell or accuse them of anything. I simply let them know how their actions affected us. We drew a healthy boundary with each of them.

It was very healing for me to share my true feelings when I had held them back for eighteen years. Nowadays, I will very kindly and very honestly tell you the truth. I am much better now that God has healed me and my responses are more tempered but never diluted unless the Holy Spirit tells me to.

GIVE YOURSELF ROOM TO HEAL

You are going to need room and time to heal especially if the hurt was deep. Don't feel rushed or allow others to rush you, but don't take forever, either. Take steps towards forgiveness every day. Make up your mind to forgive.

My husband even took it to another level. He went to the house of the person who trashed his name and he asked for forgiveness for anything he may have offended him in. Yes, he did. I was so hurt I said, "God, I just want You. I want Your will. I want Your purpose." I was willing to forgive the world, and it felt so good, but I knew we needed to distance ourselves from that particular family. This gave us room to heal.

IT'S OKAY TO SAY GOODBYE

Some hurts are so deep that you'll have to say goodbye. We were willing to forgive and even considered starting the relationship over fresh, but some weren't interested. So we went our separate ways. Danny and I did our part—we forgave and understood that it was done. We stopped pursuing people who were rejecting us. They may have not had evil intentions against us but one thing is for certain, the enemy of our soul will always attempt to use wrong information and misunderstanding to fuel the fire of accusation and defamation. Even this, God can turn into a sweet place.

> Stop chasing people who don't want anything to do with you.

Release people who don't want you in their lives. Don't waste your precious energy. Those people were done with us and we were done trying to make the relationship work. They got what they wanted and needed out of the relationship and it was time to let them go. We only harm ourselves when we constantly pursue people who want nothing to do with us.

Trust God for new relationships. Even if you are married and your spouse doesn't want you around, are they done with you? Give them room to breathe—if not, you'll make it worse. If you're always in their face, I'd recommend the book, *Love Must Be Tough*, especially when you've done all you can. [1]

IT'S OKAY TO CRY

Oh, my goodness, did I cry? I cried every day. I cried, complained, and had a pity party for years. When hundreds of people walked away from us and our church, we had to literally build brand new. Crying was a way I dealt with the level of pain we felt. It is very healing, and there's a season for it.

We eventually did rebuild with a brand-new group of people and a small remnant of those that stayed with us. These people loved us and we loved them, and those are the best kind of people to build something great with.

Almost five years later, we now have a church full of love. We can be very honest and transparent with no need to impress them because many of them are just as broken as we were. I love being a part of seeing them coming back to life again. If you are facing a rebuild in your life, remember, it's okay to cry—it's going to be better, I promise you.

time to reflect

Describe a situation in a relationship that hurt you.

Do you feel hatred towards this person?

PRAYER

Father,

Even though my heart is filled with hate towards this person, today I choose to give You this hurt and to release the person from wronging me. Today, I choose to forgive. Matthew 6:14 says, "If you forgive those who sin against you, your heavenly father will forgive you." I forgive this person who hurt me and ask for forgiveness for my own life. I claim this promise.

In Jesus' name, Amen.

chapter 8

STOP RUNNING

DON'T RUN FROM IT

We run from our brokenness,
but God runs towards our brokenness.

When I finally decided to stop running and allow all my brokenness to catch up to me, I just sat there and cried, allowing God to take my big mess. I literally put my pain on display for all to see, but most importantly, for God to see. I had a feeling it would be a testimony of God's great power and had no idea that a book would come out of it.

Broken is beautiful—don't resist what it does in your life. We think that God is not into brokenness and we tend to draw away from Him and to distance ourselves when life knocks us down. We think He has abandoned us because of our wrong decisions. No one is beyond repair. Remember, the Bible says He's near to the brokenhearted and to those who are crushed in spirit.[1] Allow God to walk you through your broken places.

BEAUTIFULLY BROKEN

I made an immediate decision to embrace that I was beautifully broken. I wanted to connect with other ladies who felt stuck in the painful part of brokenness and just pour into them, teaching them it can be beautiful even amidst all the ugliness. So many people are hurting, and like them, I was in pain, broken over my situation. I decided not to stay there and that brokenness wouldn't be my address forever, but while I was there, I allowed God to make it beautiful.

I decided to create a Facebook page and an Instagram page, and called it "Beautifully Broken Women." Immediately, it jumped to 500 followers. Since then I've changed it to our names, Daniel and Jennifer Cruz, because we have successfully moved from broken to empowered.

Worshiping with one hand and rescuing someone with the other hand, I started to come out of my shell of pain and brokenness. My eyes began to recognize the pain of others, especially pastors' wives. I shared my story without reservation. It's hard for anyone to admit they are broken inside, so I was happy for the ladies who were honest enough to say they needed help and open enough to share past or current situations.

Gleaning from my own experiences, I drew out their pain. Together we cried and prayed for one another. Sometimes, people might look at you funny when you're transitioning out of brokenness because you may be a hot mess. It's OK—don't allow that to bother you and stay right where God needs you be.

My desire was to share my message of hope and how God saw me through as much as possible. Every time I shared my story, someone got healed. But what was amazing was that I kept getting healed, too. When we start to focus on others, even when we're in pain, God brings healing.

I'M GETTING IT ALL BACK

I understood that to get my peace of mind and everything that was stolen from me back, I needed to incorporate certain things into my life. Worship was one of them, but also the rescuing of those who were hurting.

In putting my pain on display, I got all that I lost back. I knew that everyone would see the pain, but one day everyone would see the gain. Everyone would see me pregnant again carrying that baby. Everyone would see me as a happy mother of many children, both naturally and spiritually. Everyone would see me loving my man again onstage and off, proclaiming my love for him. I was proclaiming out loud like a crazy woman in my house, in my car, even at church. I was proclaiming that I was getting it all back. People would see me in my car, praying—they probably thought I was out of my mind, but I was finally in my right mind.

time to reflect

Describe a time when you experienced brokenness.

How did you respond?

Did you feel closer to God or did you feel far, far away?

PRAYER

Father,

Psalm 34:18[1] says that You're near to the brokenhearted and to those crushed in spirit. Psalm 147:32 tells me You will heal my broken heart. Today, I pray that Your peace will surround me and that even in my brokenness, I will draw closer to You. Even in the broken places of my life, I pray You help me learn to worship You and to give over to You all those pieces that are hurting.

In Jesus' name, Amen.

chapter 9

DOES EVERYONE NEED TO BE IN MY BUSINESS?

BEING OPEN ENOUGH TO BE HEALED

There will always be people who hurt us,
but there will also be people who heal us.

Our job is to allow them to do that. When I needed to stop being fake and stop acting as if everything was fine when I knew that it wasn't was one of the first steps I took to become whole again. I needed to be open enough to be healed by people whom I loved and who really loved me. Just because I was a pastor's wife, I shouldn't think that people from my church couldn't lay hands on me and pray.

I didn't need to always be strong. That was a huge lesson for me. I needed to open myself up to people who loved me in my mess, who didn't criticize me, but embraced me and prayed for me, healing me with their prayers, their love, and their experiences. It was so prideful of me to think it was only a one-way street.

When I started to trust and be open again, the people in my church could pray me back to life. I allowed them to sit and cry with me, and to send me love letters of life and hope. My spiritual children even hugged me back to life. That's what God will do—He will give you more people to love you than the ones who left you. Our church has always had a good mixture of different races. One sister at church, a big and strong, beautiful, African American, was my right hand. She would always make sure I was okay, but I always felt like I couldn't allow her or anyone else access to the deep parts of my heart.

I felt being a pastor was a job and I was their fearless and flawless leader. I've learned that God will bring you key people to be your support, and that it's okay to cry on their shoulders. How I love Freda Johnson—she loved me back to life again. Her big hugs and prayers and the look of love and support in her eyes was such a huge part of my healing.

God used so many of our spiritual children at our church to heal us. He also used other pastors who took time from their busy schedules, even on New Year's Eve, Pastors John and Noemi Figueroa left their church service to be with us on a critical night.

God used our family, especially my sister and her husband, who opened up their home to our mess and loved us without judgement.

God actually restored my relationship with my sister during this season. He knows how to make up for the hurt. You'll be amazed how many other relationships are actually healed during a broken season. You've just got to be willing to let your pride down and open your heart to people who really love you. Stop judging them as if they can't help you.

Sometimes, you need to reach rock bottom to allow God to use who He chooses to love you back to life. You can't judge them, their mistakes, or their lifestyle just because they're not perfect enough to help you and your hopeless self (I can say that because that was me). I'm not saying that just anyone can counsel you, but there are key people who, in the midst of their issues, can give your life a spark of hope and put you right back on your feet again.

They may not be the ultimate example of living right before God, but if they're trying and their heart is towards God and towards you, then allow them the space. I've known pastors who are a bit on the wild side, but one word they spoke to me during my brokenness gave me hope. I wouldn't follow their example of living or make them my new best friend, but they embraced me and cared enough to show it.

Sometimes these people may be your own crazy family members or churchgoers. You've got to be open enough to see it and receive it, and sometimes that doesn't happen until you are completely undone. If you will be open enough, the healing awaits you.

OPEN TO BROKEN PEOPLE

I used to be so judgmental about broken people. They used to irritate me with their drama ("when will they finally get over it?") and endless grumbling songs about their problems. Both my husband and I would criticize these people because we wanted them healed overnight. It wasn't until we went through brokenness ourselves that we were able to become sensitive to the brokenness of others.

I now love songs about brokenness because they carried me through my hard times. I always remind myself that I'm a worshiper, and worship is God's therapy. If I'm broken, then I will worship! I remind myself that it was God's love plus the love of others that brought me back. It was my being open enough to say I need help and being willing to reach one hand up towards God in worship and the other towards rescuing someone. I love broken people because I can now show them God's way out.

OPEN TO MY HUSBAND

As I've shared, my husband played a huge role in my healing but I needed to be open enough to allow him to be a part. I needed to be humble enough to see that God could use him. It was my husband who would pray for me. I was so oppressed by the enemy that I would tell my husband to stop praying. So he would just sit there and hold me, praying silently to himself.

He never stopped praying and believing God would use him to heal me. Actually, one text I received from Marilyn Hickey said this:

> "The enemy of your soul is also the enemy of your family, beloved daughter of Zion. Do not let the destroyer take or have his way in your marriage or in your family. God is your protector and your shield. Be sensitive to your spouse's heart, humble yourself, and be a comfort to him or her. When you are a healer, the enemy loses ground. Trust God oh daughter of Zion. Love your Boaz, who was your chosen one and your soul's delight."

My response in my journal was, "I don't know how to do this." God began to take me down a journey of learning how to allow my husband to heal me. He will do the same for you if you are willing and open enough to be healed.

time to reflect

Name a few people that came across as "wanting to be in your business" but they ended up being the people God would use to heal you. Perhaps a woman of wisdom or someone who understands God's Word?

Have you opened your heart to such people? If so, have you told them how much you love and appreciate them?

PRAYER

God, Your Word says in Proverbs 31:26: "She speaks with wisdom, and faithful instruction is on her tongue." That is the kind of woman I want to be and the kind of woman I need in my life as a friend or a mentor. Help me to be on the look out for her and if she's already in my life, then help me to always appreciate her.

In Jesus' name I pray, Amen.

chapter 10

THE DISAPPOINTING TRUTH ABOUT THIS BEAUTY QUEEN

THE DISAPPOINTMENT

Since I was a little girl, I watched all the beauty pageants on television and I would think to myself, "Can I be her? Can I do that?" That quiet little desire was always in my heart and once I moved in with my uncle and aunt, my uncle would not allow me to be part of such a thing. It wasn't until I got married that my husband told me about the "Mrs." pageants for married women. I was so thrilled. I joined the pageant industry but quickly noticed it went from being a desire to an obsession to receive all the affirmation that was missing in my life.

The year I won the title of Mrs. Illinois, United States, was the worst year of my life—yet was it? After so many years of trying and competing in different beauty pageants, longing for the affirmation and approval could only be gained by my finally breaking down and allowing God to redo my life all over again.

What I thought was the end was actually the beginning of something new.

Pageants are fun if you enter with the right motives and connect with the correct organization. I finally connected to the right one, and I would know because I've tried all of the married women's beauty pageants. I can tell you which ones operate in integrity and which ones don't.

The disappointment of spending almost ten years of my life trying to win a pageant was very stressful, but it did give me the focus I needed to keep my body on track. Every time I had a baby, I would work my behind off because I knew that the following year I would enter a pageant again.

I was so unprepared for the first pageant. I didn't even make the top ten and was convinced I should have. At least I won Mrs. Photogenic. I was actually getting tired of only winning that title—usually Mrs. Photogenic comes out in the top ten, but not me. What a disappointment.

ALWAYS A RUNNER-UP, NEVER A QUEEN

I then had a streak of getting runner-up—always runner up. After I had my second child, I tried again, and this time, I made the top five. That felt like an accomplishment. After the next baby the following year, I tried again and I won first runner-up. You'd think I'd be grateful, but I was so depressed that night and took my anger out on my dear husband. That didn't stop me, though. The following year I was at it again.

Whatever the cost to enter the pageant, the work involved to get the sponsors, or the price for all the arguments, I was willing to pay it. I have always wanted to do pageants, and I've always been a fighter. The cost of disappointments and the letdowns didn't stop me either. I needed to prove to the world, my friends, my family, and those who admired me, to everyone I was trying to impress that I would get this crown and I would win the title.

The following year, I entered again and ended up in third place. I was so devastated because I had "believed" God, declared the Word, and slapped everyone with scriptures that told me something different. My heart was so wrong. I may have been doing a good thing but it was for all the wrong reasons. Soon, it would all come crashing down.

TIME TO IMPRESS WAS OVER

I wanted to look good in other people's eyes. I wanted to impress people who weren't even interested in being impressed by me—isn't that something? I wanted to prove a point, and was looking for that constant affirmation, but my time to impress was coming to a crashing end.

I joined another organization and won the title of Mrs. Illinois, United States in 2012. I was so happy—the crown was huge and beautiful. I had different speaking engagements to attend where I waved my hand and enjoyed my crown, but I had no idea that 2012 would be the year I walked away from it all.

Walking away, stopping, quitting, pretending, and faking it all came to an end. I had so much conflict which wasn't necessarily a sign that something was wrong—it was a sign that I needed to give in. I needed to allow the pieces to fall however they may.

When you're broken, your true beauty shows through and the real you is revealed. I didn't need to be part of a pageant, I needed a genuine God-experience to completely transform my life and show me the true beauty inside. I have nothing against pageants when they are done the right way. However, I was trying to make a name for myself at any cost, and when it was all said and done, I ended up on the floor crying before God in pain.

I laid down my life at His feet, making a solid decision to chase Him more than any other crown. My husband came to realize the need I had for his affirmation in support of this strong leader God was creating me to be.

The best thing about learning from my past is knowing what not to bring into my future.

Time to Reflect

Describe a time in your life when you were exhausted of trying to impress others. Wasn't it tiring?

Galatians 1:10 says, "For am I now seeking the approval of man, or of God? If I were still trying to please man, I would not be a servant of Christ."

PRAYER

Dear Jesus,

Galatians 1:10 says it all. I don't want to live my life always trying to impress man. Yes, I'll work hard and be faithful, but trying to get the approval of man is very draining. I am Your servant and as I look to please You first every day of my life, I believe that everything else will fall into its proper place.

In Jesus' name I pray, Amen.

chapter 11

GOD GETS OVER IT,
SO MAYBE YOU SHOULD, TOO

HE WAS ACTUALLY WITH ME

I think what surprised me the most about God is that He has walked with me through all my past, my pain, and my mistakes. Even when I thought He was far away, I actually felt He was near—so weird, but so true. Many times, when we're in a season of brokenness, we assume God is far away.

It may be because we're at a place of not caring what people think about us anymore. As we start to walk in this freedom, it feels so good, but we then think God must be against it. Did you know that God so longs for you to get to that point in your life, where the only thing that matters is His opinion of you and not everyone else's?

That's what people didn't understand about me. They saw me free but in my freedom, I wasn't necessarily sugar-coating things anymore. Now, I spoke my mind freely without searching for anyone's approval. I still needed some work but God would do the work as I continued.

What held me back for years and kept my thoughts from being truly expressed was over. Quitting, being okay with quitting and being unconcerned about what others thought about me was so freeing. I've broken God's heart so many times in my life yet I never ceased to feel Him beckoning at my heart. I would find myself falling for His unconditional love all over again.

Why should we try to walk through our brokenness without God? That's when we need Him the most. Maybe it's because so many of us haven't understood the proper love of a father, so we view God based on the behavior and responses of our earthly father. If our earthly father abandoned us, then we think that God will do the same. Sometimes it's the separation sin creates that makes us feel we're not connected to God, but we need to know that God longs to hear from us.

One thing I've learned about God is that He gets over it.

He's not holding your sin and your stupid mistakes against you forever. Isaiah 54:8 says "'In a burst of anger, I turned my face away for a little while. But with everlasting love I will have compassion on you' says the Lord, your redeemer." He usually gets over it in a few days, just like any good dad would.

I remember I broke my uncle's heart when I disobeyed him. He wouldn't talk to me for a few days. His silence hurt, but it really made me think about what I had done. Sure enough, after a few days, he would come looking for me and love on me. That's just like God, and once again, our relationship was restored.

We need to get a proper understanding of God's love—the love of the Father. Yes, He may get upset when we make stupid decisions, but He gets over it, and starts looking for us again. "'For a brief moment I left you; with deep love I will take you back. I turned away angry for a moment, but I will show you my love forever,'" says the Lord who saves you."[1]

I NEVER THOUGHT IT WOULD BE SO GOOD

As I have looked over the past five years, I have asked, "Who am I?" Yes, my journey was hard; yes, I cried and wondered when this would all be over. When would the pain stop, and when would the hurt be over? I wondered if I would ever make it. I wondered when is enough, enough? I wanted all those things, but each time I was at a place of desperation, God would give me a scripture or send me a preacher or a worship song to see me through.

My Bible became my journal. I've gone through so many Bible verses. Every two years, I've had to buy a new Bible because I have been sticking my face so deep into God's Word, pulling out scriptures that would bring me back to life again—and you've got to do the same.

SO GLAD I DIDN'T STOP

I'm so glad that I didn't stop; so glad I kept pressing on, even when I was seemingly not getting anywhere. I'm so glad my heart turned back to God. I'm so glad I overcame the season of being numb, of not feeling anything and still trusted God. It reminds me of the Chinese bamboo tree that takes five years to see any growth. But once it starts to grow, during its fifth year, it grows ninety feet tall in about ninety days.

It took five years of watering that seed every day, even when I didn't see anything changing. Our problem is that we want to see everything overnight. We want our relationships healed overnight, but we're not willing to water them in prayer. We want God to be our personal little genie at our command and to rub the bottle until He comes out to grant us our wish.

He's not a genie, and it wasn't until I got serious with God that He got serious with me. I once told God, "I'll give you a year to fix this situation, this mess, this brokenness," but instead He took five. He knew how long it was going to take to detox me of me, of everything I'd intoxicated myself with. Five years of crying, five years of believing, five years of speaking God's Word over my emotions, five years of speaking life, five years of learning to go an entire week without arguing with my husband, five years of humbling myself and going to people as the Holy Spirit would lead to ask for forgiveness.

God began to show me the ugly side in my time of brokenness. He needed time for the pride and hurt to be healed and the overwhelming, overbearing person I had become to return to the life He had planned for me. With each year, the devil was losing more of his control of my life. Every time I filled out a card of apology or took a cake to someone we heard was hurt by us, I felt the chains and layers of resentment begin to fall off. What freedom—and it all came from brokenness.

THE DEVIL LOST

The devil lost. Here I am, just over five years later, in my 40's and looking like I'm in my 30's. I'm not being boastful, I'm just telling you what God did because I released all the junk I was carrying. My husband is in his early 50's, and he seriously looks like he's in his 30's, too.

God has done spiritual plastic surgery on us, repairing all the years of suffering. We allowed God to make the broken places the sweetest places. The devil lost despite all the screaming he did in my ear. He knew very well that five years later my life, my marriage, my family, and our ministry would be healthier and better than it ever was before.

I now have a new marriage with the same man, and I love him 110%. He is my hero. He's so proud of me, and he lets me be me. He's my best friend so much so that sometimes I accidentally call him "girlfriend" when I'm talking to him because I truly feel like I'm speaking to someone that close. He's so understanding. Don't get me wrong—I still want to choke him every once in a while, but I no longer want to kill him. It's so amazing to think that everything I survived and everything you've survived will one day help someone else make it, too.

time to reflect

Describe a time that you've decided to get serious with God.

What was the outcome?

If you're getting serious about having a relationship with God, the first step you need to deal with is sin. There were many times that my own heart was filled with sin, anger, bitterness, pride and hatred. I dislike writing this but it was the truth of the matter.

To say it simply, sin is anything that is not pleasing to God. There are things that are right and things that are wrong. The Bible talks about people who do what is right in their own eyes and the counsel or help of others doesn't carry much value. When a person lives their life with no concern for God's plan and purpose for their life, they will end up living a life that is filled with sin.

Isaiah 59:2 says, "But your iniquities have separated you from your God; and your sins have hidden His face from you, so that He will not hear."

If you're ready to get serious with God, then you need to find the answer to this question that is found in Acts

16:30-31, "What must I do to be saved?" The answer, "Believe on the Lord Jesus Christ, and you will be saved."

To be saved means to be set free from God's wrath or impending judgement. This is a gift that comes by faith when you believe in Jesus Christ as your Lord and Savior. How are you saved? By admitting that there is sin in your life and that this sin separates you from a holy God. This is why Jesus Christ came to live and die on the cross to take upon himself the penalty for your sins.

This first step is very important because if you have not put your faith, your belief, and your trust in Jesus Christ, you are not yet a true follower of God nor a part of his family. When you get serious about God and accept Jesus as Lord and Savior of your life you will be born again.

PRAYER

Lord Jesus,

Forgive me of all my sins. Today, I've decided to get serious with You. Come into my heart and cleanse me of all unrighteousness. I want You to be my Lord and Savior, not just today but for the rest of my life. Thank You for being my Lord.

In Your name I pray, Amen.

chapter 12

NOTHING IS OVER,
NOTHING IS TOO LATE

THE PROCESS MAY FEEL LONG

It's never too late. If you are reading this book, there is still hope. Your life matters and you do make a difference. You've come this far for a reason and nothing is over until God says it's over. It doesn't matter how ugly, how dirty, or how nasty it's been, the blood of Jesus is sufficient to wipe it all away and break every chain off your life. When you look in the mirror, you may see broken, but He sees beautiful.

Several years ago, we wanted to live in Oak Park in a beautiful vintage home. This was the home that God would use to heal our marriage and our family. We just felt like we needed a fresh start in a new place to build our life together.

We found this beautiful home that needed some painting and some care, but nothing too difficult. The home became very popular on the market, and after putting in all of our paperwork, we received a phone call that they had leased it to someone else.

We didn't stop there because we really felt it was supposed to be ours. We were still hurting emotionally, but we needed to move forward. I told Danny, "Let's go to Oak Park and pray in front of the house," so we did. That week, we contacted our agent and asked her to join us in prayer. We didn't know if she was a believer or not; we were just desperate for God to move in our situation. We gathered at the house for prayer, and three days later she received a phone call that the lease had been broken by the other party involved and the house was ours!

Believe what God has for you, because it's yours. Had we settled and not prayed or called back, we wouldn't have gotten the home. Let me be clear: no one had yet bought the home that we were praying over. Many times, we see something that belongs to someone else and we think we can pray and take it—that's called covetousness.

The Bible is clear about not coveting your neighbor's house or your neighbor's wife. If that man is married, he's not yours; if that house belongs to someone else and is not for sale or for rent, then it's not yours. We just need to be careful when we're praying. In this case, three days later the house was released because we prayed, we believed, and we declared in faith that it would be ours. We moved in May, and after a couple of months, started painting and decorating it into a beautiful home of restoration.

GOD FOUGHT WHEN I COULDN'T

We moved into our beautiful Victorian home with a pink phone in the kitchen and the farmhouse table in the dining room. All the trips to the resale shop, all the Pinterest ideas, all the drives to pick up shabby chic things from Craigslist, and even a drive to Florida to visit other resale shops brought glorious healing to us. We had no idea healing could come this way.

I started taking long walks through Oak Park. I wondered how long the entire healing process would take. God started to heal our family, or better said, we *allowed* God to heal our family, but I remember wondering, "How long is it going to take?" I felt like I would be in the process forever. I didn't know what was going to happen and began to question whether He was really walking with me. Deep down inside, I knew that He was with me, that he was listening to me and walking with me. I didn't know what the full process was going to look like.

I had no idea that those walks every morning, every evening, and even in the afternoon were going to be the road to my healing— the road He would use to restore my life. I want to encourage you because sometimes you're on that road to restoration in the process of healing, still asking, "God, how long is it going to take? Are you really walking with me, or am I walking in this journey alone?" I want to encourage you because God can use a walk to heal you; He can use a drive to heal you.

With tears in my eyes, I would say, "God, I don't understand. I feel alone, but I know You are with me." It's in that journey, that the process of healing takes place. I ended up opening a little boutique, a resale shop in my garage. My husband helped me decorate it. During all the times of just sitting there, taking all those walks back and forth, or filling up my little boutique, God was restoring my soul as I was crying out to Him. I'm in such a better place today. I know I'm healed.

Healing takes time, so don't feel rushed. Sometimes the things God needs to do takes time sitting at His feet, walking, praying, or wondering if He's hearing you. The process and the journey to complete healing are so important.

Today, I cherish those walks with God because they helped to develop my faith. I'm stronger now than I've ever been before. I am not easily moved or shaken any more. I'm not bothered by other people's issues or brokenness. I'm at peace with my life and with where I'm at.

God has healed my life and given me the grace to start over, the grace to start a new love with my husband who is now my best friend whom I simply adore and love doing life with. God gave us both the grace to start over, building a new church with those who walked us through our brokenness.

We both have grown more in the last five years than in the eighteen years before. My beautiful children have been restored from all the arguments and the pain of separation. We're not a perfect family, but we are perfectly in love with each other. I can now say that I'm so thankful for all the broken places in my life because I've allowed them to produce sweetness, and my prayer for you is that you'll do the same. Don't get bitter—get better because greatness will come out of your season of brokenness

Have you grown from your season of brokenness?
Has this book helped you to see how it can all be turned around?

Do you know of someone that can benefit from choosing sweetness over bitterness?

If so, would you do them a huge favor and tell them about this book? Together you and I can see thousands come to a place of freedom and restoration.

I'm praying for you,

Love,

Jennifer

about the author

Jennifer Jordan Cruz, a Chicago native and former Mrs. Illinois, is an outstanding and prolific speaker. She mentors and teaches on the power to prevail in life as a wife, mother, business woman and co-pastor.

She candidly shares her personal journey from brokenness to triumph and provides encouragement to thousands so they can experience this dynamic shift as well. She is a sought-after conference speaker and has a large social media following for her Live Wednesday Morning Prayers on Facebook and Instagram.

Jennifer has authored two other books: *I Just Had a Baby* and *Easy Peasy Potty Training Tips and Tricks*. In addition, Jennifer has launched several business ventures including a jewelry store, a boutique in her garage, and an outdoor wedding venue. She models the fact that opportunity is always within reach if you eliminate excuses and step out in faith.

All of her business ventures help support missions around the world. She co-pastors Faithworld Church in Chicago alongside her husband, Pastor Daniel Cruz, the love of her life, for over 25 years. Together, they have five precious children: Faith, Aaron, Kaitlyn, Ethan, and an older adopted daughter, Elcira.

JenniferJordanCruz.com

INVITE JENNIFER TO SPEAK

To inquire about having Jennifer speak at your church or upcoming event, email her team at:

PastorJenniferCruz@gmail.com

ENDNOTES

INTRODUCTION

1. Ecclesiastes 3:1
2. Psalm 34:18 NIV

CHAPTER 1

1. Isaiah 61:3
2. Psalm 27:10
3. Jeremiah 29:11 NIV
4. Ruth 2-4

CHAPTER 2

1. Proverbs 13:20

Chapter 3

1. Psalm 139:14 NIV
2. Psalm 118:17 NKJV

CHAPTER 4

1. 1 Peter 5:7

CHAPTER 6

1. Proverbs 31:28
2. "Break Every Chain" by Tasha Cobbs

CHAPTER 7

1. Dobson, James. *Love Must Be Tough: New Hope for Families in Crisis.* Word Books: 1983.

CHAPTER 8

1. Psalm 34:18
2. Psalm 147:3
Chapter 11
1. Isaiah 54:7-9 GNT

WORKS CITED

The Bible. Good News Translation. *BibleGateway.com.* Zondervan, 2008.

http://gateway.com. Accessed 22 February 2018.

The Bible. New International Version. *BibleGateway.com.* Zondervan, 2008.

http://gateway.com. Accessed 22 February 2018.

The Bible. New King James Version. *BibleGateway.com.* Zondervan, 2008.

http://gateway.com. Accessed 22 February 2018.

Dobson, James. *Love Must Be Tough: New Hope for Families in Crisis.* Word Books: 1983.

All scriptures are taken from the New International Version of the Bible unless otherwise noted.